THE COMPLETE
FROG

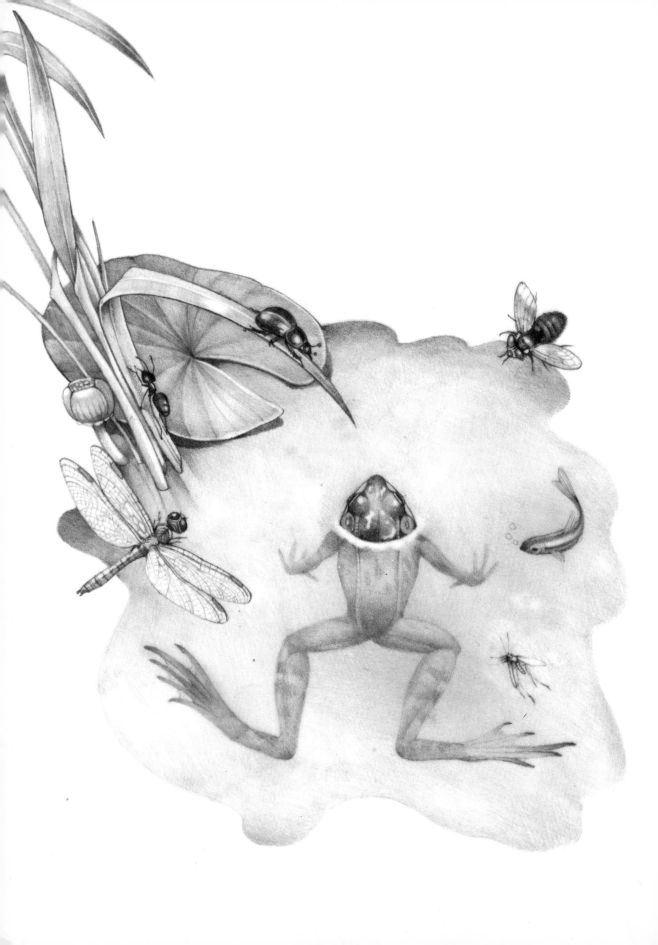

THE COMPLETE
FROG

A Guide For The Very Young Naturalist

BY ELIZABETH A. LACEY

ILLUSTRATED BY CHRISTOPHER SANTORO

LOTHROP, LEE & SHEPARD BOOKS/NEW YORK

For
Jebby Florence and Donald II
with love

E.A.L.

For
Tara and Barbara

C.S.

First Edition   1   2   3   4   5   6   7   8   9   10

Library of Congress Cataloging in Publication Data
Lacey, Elizabeth A. The complete frog.
Bibliography: p.   Includes index. Summary: Explores the world of the frog, examining its physical characteristics, life cycle, eating habits, and place in fact and fiction. 1. Frogs—Juvenile literature. [1. Frogs] I. Santoro, Christopher, ill. II. Title. QL668.E2L23 1989   597.8'9   88-9343
ISBN 0-688-08017-0 ISBN 0-688-08018-9 (lib. bdg.)

43018

"All told, in habitats from all climates, the Class Amphibia scores three-thousand species, just as many as the total number of non-flying mammals. We're not living in the Age of Mammals, we're living in the Age of Frogs."

Robert T. Bakker, Ph.D.
The Dinosaur Heresies

Contents

1.
What a Frog Is

No fins, no fangs, no feathers, no fur. When you stop to think about it, the ''ordinary'' frog is not such an ordinary animal at all.

For one thing, these small creatures represent a truly extraordinary story of survival success: They are among the few remaining members of the oldest family of land-dwelling animals on earth—a family named Amphibia (am-FIB-e-uh) that first appeared even before there were any dinosaurs.

Science tells us the humble frog's ancestors were true pioneers, being the first creatures to survive the drying up of the vast ancient oceans by crawling onto land and developing the ability to breathe through lungs.

It is also believed that those earliest amphibians brought vocal sound as we know it into the world. Before them there had been only the mechanical whirring and buzzing of insects.

Eryops

An insect makes noise with its external body parts, often just by moving about.

With amphibians came sound from the throat controlled by the animal itself and serving a purpose among the members of a group.

One of the best-known amphibian ancestors is Eryops (AIR-ee-ops), a beast often as much as seven feet long. We know about Eryops from fossils, the animal's bones that turned to stone during the millions of years since it died.

Fossilized frogs are quite rare, not only because the small bones are liable to break up, but also because frogs tend to be eaten rather than left to fossilize. Even so, a few have been found beautifully preserved in rocks said to be some 10 million years old.

The word *amphibian* is from the Greek language and means those animals that are as much at home in water as on land.

Our word *frog* comes to us from the English. In the days of King Arthur these small, green fellows were called *frogga*. By the time of Robin Hood it had become *frogge*. However, according to a book available in England about fifty years before Columbus set sail to discover America, *frogge* was supposed to mean the creature we now call a toad. *Froke* was given as the word for today's frog.

If you are a frog-fancying person, you already know that while frogs and toads are similar in many ways, they are not identical. You might sum it up by calling them cousins because both are amphibians.

Scientists called paleontologists (pay-lee-en-TOL-o-jists) look for and study the bones of long-dead animals. They say that 300 million years ago there were many kinds of amphibians on earth. Today there are only three kinds of true amphibians.

One is the Gymnophiona (jim-no-FIE-owna) or caecilian (see-SILLY-ann) order, made up of blind, wiggly, legless creatures easily mistaken for worms.

The second order is called Urodela (ura-DEE-la) or Caudata (caw-DATA), meaning "tailed ones." These are the newts and salamanders which, with four legs and long tails, tend to look a lot like lizards.

The third order is identified as Anura (AN-ur-a) or Salientia (sally-ENCH-a), "jumping ones." This is the order that includes frogs and toads, and it has more members, so far as naturalists have been able to tell, than both of the other two put together.

These salientians have a highly distinctive appearance. Having seen them once, you will easily recognize them next time, and you would never mistake one of them for anything else.

It is telling them one from the other that gets a little tricky.

Gymnophiona

Anura

Urodela

13

2.
Frog or Toad: How to Tell

Frogs and toads have the same overall shape and often seem much alike in color and habits. Both of these amphibians, for instance, usually lay their eggs in or near water.

Generally speaking, if you find it in a pond it is the common frog, and if you find it in the woods it is the common toad, but there are other clues as well.

green frog

American

The Common Frog

Smooth, soft skin

Long ridges down each side
of back

Largish round "ears" under
eyes on each side

Slender body, long legs,
speedy swimmer

Lives in or very near water

Small teeth in upper jaw only

Clumps of eggs laid in water

Male has eardrums larger than
eyes

The Common Toad

Thick, bumpy skin

Short ridges on top of head,
largish bumps behind eyes

Very small round "ears"
below eyes

Plump body, shorter legs,
slower moving

Lives on land in woods

No teeth

Strands of eggs laid in water

Male usually has dark toes
and throat

Toads differ from frogs in another interesting way.

Where you find one frog you can confidently expect to find a lot more. Even rather small ponds are able to support surprisingly large numbers of frogs.

Not so with toads. You can find one or perhaps two toads in a section of woods and have to walk quite a long way before you turn up another.

Naturalists have wondered: Does this mean frogs are more sociable than toads? Maybe. Or it may be that because frogs are so much more dependent on water, they have to put up with the company of all those other frogs, like it or not.

Some three thousand kinds of frogs and toads have been identified, and new ones continue to turn up from time to time. Because there are some few frogs with bumpy skin and some few toads that are smooth—to name only one of the complications—naturalists had to have a precise way of deciding who's who.

It happens that there are certain differences between the skeletons of frogs and toads, and scientists base their decision on that information.

For those of us who do not have an X-ray machine handy, the more obvious differences will do in most cases.

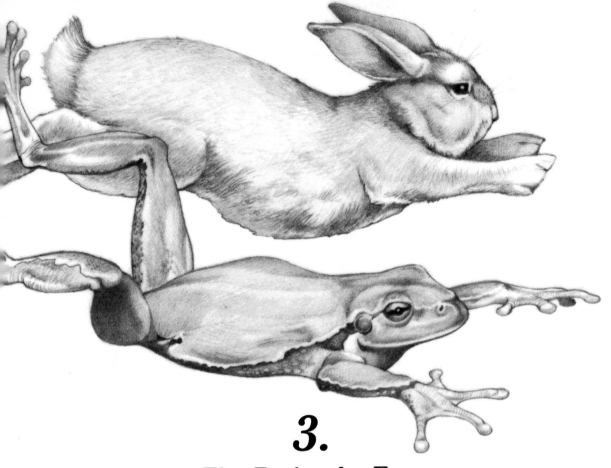

3.

The Body of a Frog

Although they may not look so from the outside, frogs are in many ways simplified miniatures of much larger animals. Just as it is possible to make several recipes using the same ingredients in different ways, so it is with living "ingredients." A frog is unique among the world's life forms, even those with which it shares the same basic structure.

It is by understanding how all life forms on our planet are alike and unalike that we can learn to care best for them and for ourselves as well.

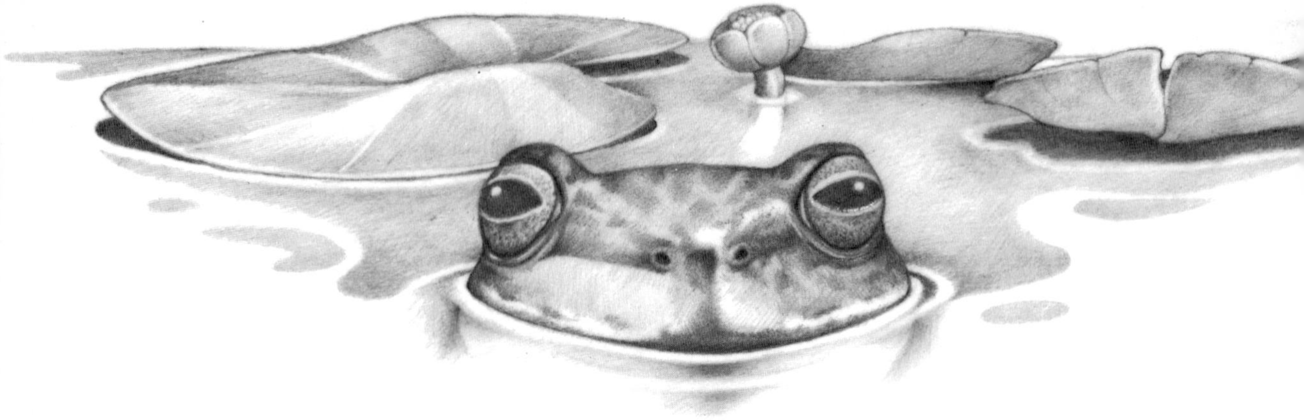

One of the things you notice first about a frog is that pair of big eyes on top of its head, one at each side. This may look odd to you, but it is very useful to the frog, which can have its entire body safely underwater and still be able to see above the surface.

When the frog dives, a clear inner eyelid closes—from the bottom up—to protect the tender eye while allowing the frog to see perfectly well.

inner eyelid clos

leopard frog

By observing the animal, naturalists have come to believe a frog can see clearly only those things that are very close. The wide placement of the eyes lets it see in almost a complete circle around itself without having to turn its head or neck. This is important because a frog does not hunt for its food. It simply picks out a spot and waits for something tasty to fly or crawl by within reach of its tongue.

spring peeper

Your tongue is fastened inside your mouth at the lower back. A frog's tongue is fastened at the lower front, so it can stick out as far as possible, enabling the frog to catch its food.

To eat, a frog flicks out its long, sticky tongue and snares its supper. Occasionally the animal may also use its front feet to grasp an especially large morsel, but most often that tongue gets the job done and gets it done very quickly. Should you be watching when a frog picks off a nearby bug, it will happen so fast you won't see the tongue itself at all.

You have a great many teeth in your upper and lower jaws and use them to chew your food. A frog swallows its food whole and has only one set of very tiny teeth in its upper jaw. These serve merely as grippers to be sure dinner doesn't get away.

Your nose sticks out above your mouth and can be seen easily. A frog's nose is just two small holes which can hardly be seen at all.

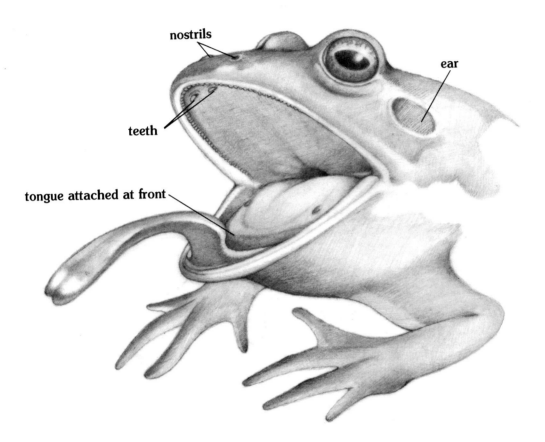

nostrils

ear

teeth

tongue attached at front

You also have highly visible ears on either side of your head. A frog has only two round, flat areas of very thin skin, called membranes, which vibrate when sound strikes them.

Though certainly not as impressive as yours, the frog's little nose and ears seem to serve equally well in letting the frog know what is going on around it.

Just as each type of bird has its own special song, so each kind of frog has a different call. The tiny spring peeper is noted for its small, clear sound, while the big bullfrog is known by its deep "jurr-rrum."

Basically, however, all frogs vocalize in the same manner. When a frog "speaks," it draws air out of its lungs and

into an air sac. Some frogs have just one large sac under the chin; others have a pair of smaller sacs, one on each side of the neck. Incoming air fills the sac (or sacs) like a bubble. The frog then flexes its throat muscles, forcing the air out of the bubble, over the vocal cords, and back into the lungs. It is the air passing over the vocal cords on the return trip that creates the frog's voice. This interesting system means that, unlike a human being, a frog is able to "talk" on and on without ever opening its mouth.

Why would a frog need to "talk" at all?

Naturalists have found that frogs use their voices during the mating, or egg-laying, season to call to one another, but that is not the only reason.

Frogs use their voices to warn one another of approaching danger and to let it be known among themselves if one thinks another has invaded private territory. They may even

be "talking about the weather"; naturalists know that frog calls also accompany the arrival of storms.

While frogs seem to understand each other's different remarks quite well, to you all their sounds may be very much the same. One sound, however, is unlike the rest. A truly terrified frog will scream, a high-pitched sound that reminds some of a baby's cry. And when one frog does emit that call of ultimate fear, the result is to instantly silence the chorusing of all the others.

As you grow, your skin stretches, producing new cells

so it grows larger as you do. As a frog grows, its skin does not stretch in the same way as yours. It splits and the frog sheds it, revealing a whole new skin underneath. This also happens to snakes, which rub off the dry old skin as they slither over rough ground. A frog has to pull off its old skin, and like some lizards will then go on to eat it.

A frog's skin is also different from yours in that it is usually two separate colors. It is dark on the frog's back so the animal blends in with the ground or water when seen from above. The skin is pale over the stomach to blend with the light surface of the water when the swimming frog is seen from below. A frog's skin reacts visibly to available light, becoming bright in sunshine and turning darker in shadows. All of this helps make the frog harder to see by those who might want to eat it—and by those the frog may be hoping to eat.

Your tough skin is a barrier between you and disease. If that barrier is broken by a cut or other wound, germs can enter your system and cause trouble. The same thing can happen to a frog.

Even though a frog's skin is equipped to protect it from some infections, there *are* serious amphibian illnesses. One such serious disease of frogs is called "red leg" because the pale underskin turns pinkish. The frog cannot give its sickness to you, but the animal itself can die of it.

You will never see a frog drink with its mouth. It has no need to, as it absorbs water through its skin. For this reason the frog must remain close to water all its life. If it becomes too hot, the frog can dry out and die in a matter of hours.

Frogs, along with toads, snakes, and lizards, are called "cold-blooded" because their bodies respond very directly to changes in the surrounding climate. Frogs that live in what are called temperate zones—places with four seasons in a year—are active in the warm spring and summer. In autumn they dig into the muddy bottom of a pond and "sleep" underground until spring returns. During this time the frog remains completely motionless, and because its body needs very little air while it is so still, it is even able to breathe through its marvelous skin.

Will the frog die if the pond freezes over? Probably not. Enough air will remain in the layer of water between the muddy bottom and the ice on top to serve the inactive frog's limited needs. Should the pond freeze solid, however, and

27

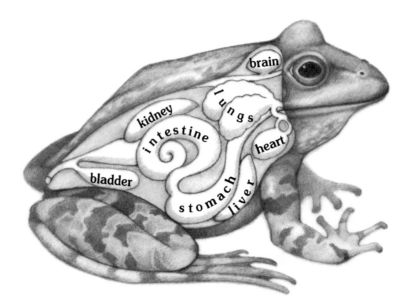

stay that way long enough, the frog might well die from a combination of too much cold and too little air.

Under its skin a frog has many of the same organs as any other animal. It has a heart to pump its blood, a stomach and intestines to process its food, lungs for breathing, a liver and kidneys to cleanse its body fluids. It also has a bladder, and when a frog is picked up suddenly it is not unusual for the bladder to "let go" on whoever is holding the animal.

And, yes, a frog has a brain, although, as you can see, it is quite small. Your enormous brain is a storehouse for an unlimited amount of information. A frog's far smaller brain is able to store only the essential facts it needs to survive. You learn a great many things quickly and with little effort, but to teach a frog even something simple requires much time, repetition, and patience. Your puppy will learn its own name and come when you call it. You could own a frog for a lifetime and it would never be able to do that. In a frog's very limited brain there is just no place to put that kind of information.

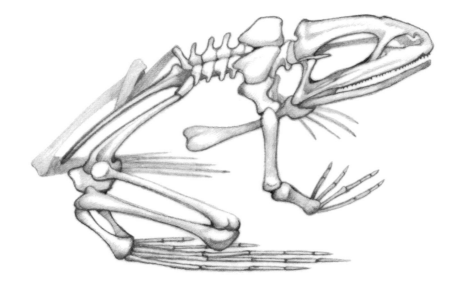

This is a frog's skeleton. Look at it closely for a moment to see if you can spot something missing, something you *would* see in the bone structure of other animals, especially mammals. That's right: A frog has no ribs, which explains why it feels so soft when held in your hand.

You can see the long leg bones. When fully stretched, a frog's hind legs are longer than all the rest of its body. Strong muscles on those legs make it possible for the frog to jump great distances. In one leap it can easily cover many times its own length.

Now count the toes on the frog's front feet. Then count the toes on the back feet. Right again: A frog has only four toes on each front foot but five on each foot in back. Also, the back feet are much larger than those in front to serve a special purpose. Occasionally a frog will use its front feet as paws, to grasp something or to balance when walking; but the back feet, webbed like those of a duck, form powerful flippers for strong swimming.

Swimming, of course, is something a frog does quite well. When those long rear legs with their big paddle feet are drawn up and pushed out again quickly time after time, they propel the frog's smooth, slender body through water very rapidly. The front feet are not used in speed swimming but are kept close to the body so the streamlined frog can shoot along at a good clip when necessary. When the frog is simply floating at ease, those back legs relax into a pair of Ls and the front legs extend at either side. The frog will then stroke idly with all four feet, "treading water" to hold its position.

Frogs seldom get entirely out of water and have little reason to do so. The frog's food, drink, and protection usually depend on its staying *in* the water. When it does come up on land, the frog most often gets about by hopping, but it may use a kind of low, creeping walk. Given the way it is built, no other kind of walk would be possible for a frog.

Just about any animal you can think of is equipped with a very effective natural weapon. Snakes have fangs. Rhinoceroses, elephants, and goats have tusks or horns. Horses and zebras are among those able to kill with powerful hooves. Lions, bears, and even your dog or cat are only some of the many that rely on sharp teeth and claws in an emergency. The common frog has nothing of the sort.

A few frogs are able to give off a bad-smelling, bad-tasting fluid from their bodies if threatened. In some cases this fluid is capable of killing a small animal or stunning a larger one. Most of these frogs live in hot jungle areas and are easily recognized by their brilliant colors. They are the exceptional ones, however, for most frogs have no weapon at all.

Of course, other animals frequently fight among themselves. This is something frogs seldom do. Male bullfrogs have been seen wrestling, standing on their hind legs and grappling each other with the short forepaws much like human wrestlers, but they do each other no injury. As soon as one has pinned the other down, the winner stands back and the loser goes his way with no hurt more serious than wounded dignity.

So how *does* a frog meet what might be a life-threatening situation? Some will puff up their bodies in an apparent effort to discourage the enemy by looking too big to be swallowed. More often the unarmed frog will simply stand stock-still, seeming to hope it will go unnoticed. Sometimes it may "play dead," which is not playing at all, for when severely frightened a frog can "faint" into a state where it looks quite dead.

Most of the time, however, a frog must rely on being able to swim away quickly into hiding. Speed and obscurity are really all frogs have with which to defend their lives.

4.

Frog Babies and How They Grow

You began life as an egg inside the body of your mother. You remained there until you developed all the features you have now. When you were born, you already looked like a human being. No one would have mistaken you for a giraffe or a raccoon or anything else.

Not all creatures produce their babies in that way. In many cases the mother lays eggs and young hatch from them later. While the eggs of one animal may look like those of another, the babies as they emerge resemble their parents.

With frogs the process is most often different from both of these.

Frog babies, called tadpoles, are born in the spring. They hatch from eggs laid by females in or very near water, for one way or another the eggs of most frogs must be kept moist.

When the female is ready to lay her eggs, the male clings to her back. As the eggs come from the mother's body, they are fertilized (made hatchable) by sperm from the male.

Most frogs do not raise their babies or even tend their eggs as so many other animal parents do. There are some exceptions, frogs who guard or carry the eggs until they hatch, but even with those, care most often stops as soon as the young appear. As a rule, frog parents produce their eggs and swim away, never to see their young again.

Generally frog eggs are no bigger than the periods on this page and are coated with a clear, thick jelly "shell." They sink to the bottom of the pond or stream at first. Then the jelly swells up and the eggs float back to the surface, where you may see them as a pale froth among the weeds or scum at the water's edge.

Frog eggs are a popular food for turtles, fish, and some large insects, and many are eaten before they can hatch. This is just as well, since one mother and father frog can produce several thousand fertile eggs at a time. If they all hatched and grew up, in a very little while the world would have far more frogs than it could feed.

The tadpole that comes from the egg does not look anything like the frog it will become; it is just a head and a tail. It swims about, eating small water plants and breathing through gills like a fish. The tadpole stores fat in its tail, and should the tail be bitten off by a fish or turtle the tadpole will soon grow another one.

If all goes well, however, little by little the tail will shrink as the tadpole absorbs the nutrition from it. At this time the tadpole first grows a pair of hind legs, then a pair of front legs. Meanwhile, the gills gradually close over as the animal develops the lungs that will enable it to breathe outside of water.

When the tail is finally gone, what remains is a froglet or infant frog, a perfect miniature of its kind.

How long the whole process from egg to baby frog will take depends on the type of frog it is. Some frog eggs hatch tadpoles in a couple of days, others need closer to a month. For bullfrogs the next step, going from tadpole to frog, takes a year, while smaller frogs need only a few weeks.

5.
What They Eat

The only time in its life when a frog eats plants is as a tadpole, when it dines on the weeds and other leafy growth in the water where it was hatched. Once it begins to make the change from tadpole to frog, it lives on the nutrition stored in its tail. When the tail is gone, so is the tadpole, and in its place is the fully developed froglet, which most often specializes in eating insects.

Many of the insects a frog consumes in great numbers are serious pests to human beings, such as grasshoppers and beetles that destroy food crops, and the flies, roaches, and mosquitoes that spread deadly diseases.

How does a frog know what will be a good meal for it? Naturalists have decided the answer is movement. A frog recognizes dinner by the hopping or flitting or wriggling. With few exceptions, a frog will not eat anything that is already dead.

The very smallest frogs eat the smallest insects. Larger frogs add to their diet such things as worms, moths, beetles, slugs, and snails, as well as small fish and small snakes. The very largest frogs eat all of those and have been known to include mice as well. They will eat smaller frogs, too.

As you can see, the list of things a frog will eat is very long. Longer still is the list of things that will eat frogs. Fish, turtles, and many kinds of water bugs eat frog eggs, tadpoles, and baby frogs. Full-grown frogs are eaten by owls, herons, and many other kinds of birds.

Still the list goes on. Frogs are eaten by large snakes and large fish, by otters, raccoons, shrews, minks, skunks, rats, hedgehogs, and yes, by people.

Many human beings consider frogs' legs a great delicacy, and you will find them on the menus of restaurants everywhere. In fact, so popular are frogs' legs as a human food that to meet the demand frog farms raise frogs specifically to be eaten.

Because frogs are so delicious to so many efficient hunters, it is not surprising to learn that their lives are seldom very long. There are reports of frogs that have lived ten years or more, but those were in some protected environment such as a zoo or laboratory. On its own in the wild, the average frog would be exceptionally lucky indeed to live even half that long.

6.
Looking for Frogs

You will frequently read that frogs are nocturnal, meaning they stay hidden by day and are active at night. This does not mean you won't be able to find plenty of them during the day. Far from it. Frog-watching is a very pleasant way to pass the time on a summer afternoon. You do not need a lot of expensive equipment or years of special training. All you need is sharp eyesight, patience, and some understanding of where and how to look.

Frogs will gather near any sizable body of water, in or near streams, creeks, ponds, rivers—even a large rain puddle. In general you will not find many frogs around public beaches or places with a lot of boats forever coming and going. Occasionally a frog or two may wander into such an area, but that is rare. Your best bet is a quiet backwater on a large lake or river or some little pond in the woods, not much frequented by boaters or bathers.

If you look closely as you approach, you may see great numbers of frogs sunning themselves in the shallows. More often—thanks to their coloring, which blends into the background—you will only see the plopping splashes and maybe hear their danger-warning call as they quickly vanish into the safety of deeper water. No matter how quiet you try to be, they know you are coming. However, if you find a place well away from the water's edge and sit down, taking care to cast no shadow in their direction, they will return. Remain perfectly still and perfectly quiet. It may take a while, but the frogs will gradually come back. They will likely not come too close, though, and should you move or make any noise they will promptly dive again.

If you have it in mind to catch a frog, there are some important things to think about first.

1. *Never pursue a frog into the water.* It will head for the deepest place, and you have no way of knowing just how deep that may be or what else is out there. If you are dealing with a frog in a big puddle, it may try to hide by burrowing into the soft bottom. If you go after it you are going to get terribly muddy. You may not mind, but whoever does your laundry may be annoyed.

2. *Be sure you have no insect repellent on your han*   *. . .* *you pick up a frog.* The chemicals in repellent can dam*.* the animal's skin, much as they could damage your   *.s* it you breathed in a quantity of it. Wash your hands with soap and water before you go frog hunting.

3. If you have a small net to use, fine, but frogs can be caught barehanded.

4. To carry your frog a short distance, wrap it in a wet cloth. For a longer distance you need a container with holes in the lid and plenty of wet paper towels on the bottom. The frog's skin must be kept cool and moist; if it gets hot and dry, the animal will quickly die.

Take your frog back to the place where you caught it and release it as soon as possible after capture. This gives the animal its best chance to survive the adventure of having met you.

If you plan to take a frog home, there are several very important requirements to consider.

Housing

You should keep your frog in a well-aired, glass-sided aquarium equipped with a "pond," a container of water large enough for the frog to swim in. The pond should be easily removable, so you can rinse it and provide clean water regularly. Around the pond place rocks and soil so the frog can come out of the water if it chooses and still find a place to hide. Top the aquarium with a fine mesh screen held securely in place. Do not keep the aquarium where it is in strong, direct sunlight all the time or it will get too hot.

Food

Your frog will need a continuous supply of live meals, insects or worms, of a size in keeping with the frog's size. These can be released into the aquarium and the frog will help itself when hungry. In good weather you may be able to find enough food in your own neighborhood to meet the frog's needs, but over winter—or if you live in a city—it will be a different matter. Before you bring a frog home, be sure some handy pet store sells live insects and/or worms (not all of them do) because your frog will not eat dead ones.

Care

Your frog will not need attention every day, but it will need *consistent* care. If you are going away for a few days, just give it fresh food and water before you leave. If no one will be home for a week or more, you need a "frog sitter."

Dealing with a tadpole is trickier. If you have captured one with no legs, it will need deeper water to live in and probably water plants to eat. One *with* legs will not eat anything and will live by absorbing the stored nutrition in its tail.

Either way, the tadpole's container must be equipped with a "beach," a sloping end where it can crawl out of the water. Without that feature the tadpole may not complete its development, or if it does, the new baby frog can drown if it is unable to get onto dry land.

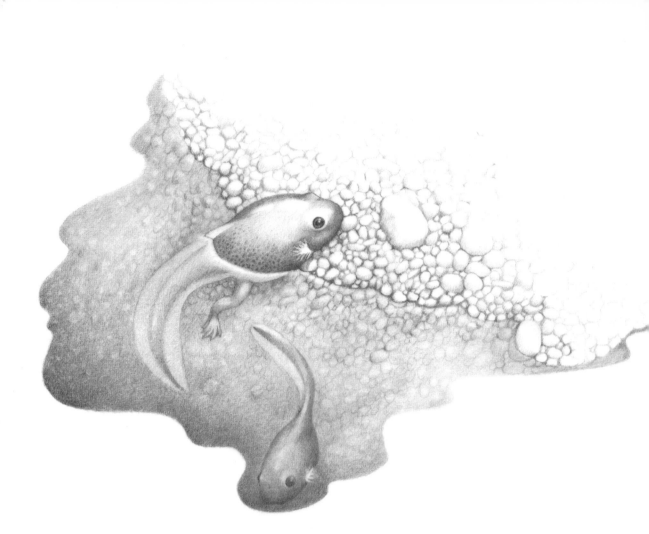

This may not sound too difficult. Tadpoles, however, look very much alike. You may not know if you have one that will need a year to become a frog or one that needs only a few weeks, and you run the risk of not having the proper environment ready at the proper time. It is also possible that

your tap water is not suitable for tadpoles because of the chemicals used in processing it. In any case, once the transformation into a baby frog is complete, remember that the living quarters and food supply have to change as well.

If you choose to keep a frog, plan to deal with it as you would a pet fish, to enjoy by looking rather than by touching. Frogs do not do well if they are handled a lot. Their delicate skin can pick up harmful substances from your hands and simply the excitement of being played with by a giant—you— may leave the little animal so terrified it cannot eat.

If you truly want to study frogs, do as real naturalists do. Go where the frogs are, follow them with your eyes, record your findings in a notebook, take pictures if you can use a camera—and in the end go home and leave them in peace. In his excellent book *The World of the Frog and the Toad* author George Porter said it best: "Wild animals are not toys."

7.

The Odd Fellows

*E*very animal family has its uncommon members, those who truly belong to the family yet who look or act very different from most of the others. There are, for instance, fish that "fly" and any number of birds that do not.

The common frog family certainly has its share of uncommon members.

Within the Salientia branch of amphibians there are, among others, the Ranidae (RANA-day), or ranids for short, and the Hylidae (HI-liday) or hylids.

Ranids are called the "true frogs." They spend almost their whole lives in water.

Hylids are better known as tree frogs. These nimble little fellows live among grass and bushes often rather far from water. You can easily recognize a hylid by its toes, which have round pads on the ends. The pads work like suction cups for

painted reed frog

49

climbing, and they grip a surface so firmly that a tree frog can creep right straight up a glass wall.

Ranids and hylids are only two of the many frog families on earth, but they are the two you will most likely find close by if you live in an area that has a cycle of four seasons through the year.

The only places on earth where you cannot find frogs are those where the weather is *always* very cold or *always* very dry. The key word there is *always* because in the amazing frog family are some wonderful relatives, able to do things and to live in places that may seem most unfroggish indeed. These relatives have developed special ways of coping with the world around them. Most live in what are called tropical countries, where the weather is both wet and warm for all or most of the year. Such places also offer plenty of dense jungle where frogs can hide and lots of insects for them to eat. Given such ideal conditions, it is no wonder that some spectacular cousins emerge.

arrow poison frogs

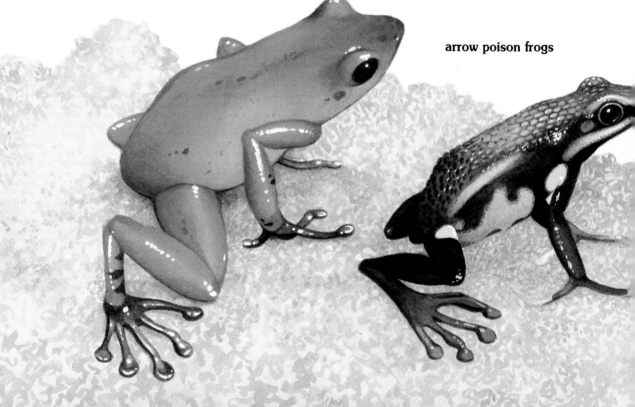

ARROW POISON FROGS of South America come in a rainbow of bright color combinations. A liquid from their skin, which serves the frog itself as a natural defense, is used by humans on arrow tips. Rather like a chemical animal tranquilizer, the fluid is able to stun prey the arrow alone would not stop.

BARKING FROGS are found in the southern United States and can be recognized by their call. They sound more like small dogs than frogs. Among these frogs the fathers stand guard over the eggs until the baby frogs emerge ready to fend for themselves.

BONY-HEADED TREE FROGS of South and Central America are surprising not only for their hostile appearance. These are among the several kinds of frogs called "marsupial" for their kangaroo-like trait of incubating their young on the mother's body.

FLAT-HEADED FROGS live in central Australia, an area that is a true desert most of the time. During the short, rare rainy spells these frogs absorb the precious water into their skins and store it as in a bag. Retreating underground when their world dries out, they are said to be able to stay buried for as long as ten years, coming back to the surface when rain returns and starting the process over again.

FLYING FROGS of Borneo are amazing members of the acrobatic tree frog clan. When the need arises, they can launch themselves out of a tree with feet spread, using their webbing as parachutes to make a safe landing well out of danger.

GLASS FROGS of Central America are so called for their remarkable transparent skin. Looking from the under-side, it is possible to actually see the frog's internal organs. One naturalist reported he was able to watch the animal's heart beating.

HAIRY FROGS of Africa do something no other frogs ever do: During the mating season males grow hair in a fancy "skirt" at their hips. Naturalists have not agreed on just what purpose this serves, but there must be one, or the trait would not continue passing from generation to generation.

HORNED FROGS of South America are noted for nasty tempers. Their horns are only a warning, being just pointed bits of skin. These frogs have very sharp teeth, however, and will not hesitate to inflict a painful bite on anything that threatens them, no matter how big it is.

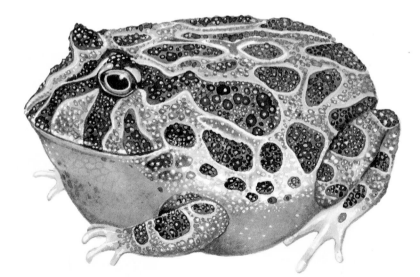

PARADOXICAL FROGS of Trinidad are unlike any others in that they actually shrink as they "grow up." Tadpoles of these frogs can be over a foot long, but after their legs sprout they get smaller and smaller until they are "full grown" at a mere 1½″ long.

RED-EYED TREE FROGS of Central America offer a brilliant contrast to the dark eyes of most other frogs. Small enough to perch on the dial of a wristwatch, these little fellows can leap considerable distances when alarmed. In doing so they display flashes of their distinctive green, white, and yellow coloring.

TAILED FROGS of the American Pacific Northwest are the only frogs known among which males keep a little stub of their tadpole tails all their lives.

TONGUELESS FROGS can be found in South America and Africa. They live completely in water, where they seldom get live insects and feed instead on what they find dead at the bottom of their lake. Obviously they do not really need a fast, sticky tongue as other frogs do.

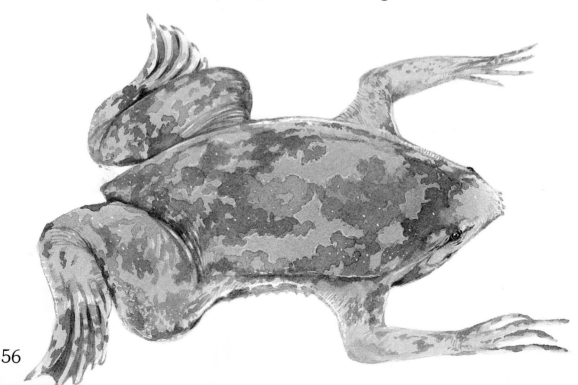

The biggest frogs in the world are probably the Goliath frogs of Africa, which have been known to measure over thirty inches in length and to weigh more than seven pounds—larger than some healthy newborn humans.

Among the very smallest frogs in the world are the Cuban arrow poison frogs, which never grow larger than one-half inch long. These also differ from other frogs in that they lay only one egg at a time. When it hatches, what appears is not a tadpole but a perfect froglet less than one-eighth inch long.

Cuba is also home to the largest known member of the genus *Hyla*: the giant tree frog. This "giant" grows to no more than five inches long, which gives you an idea of how small most hylids are.

It is not possible to know *exactly* how many frogs there are on earth at any given moment because counting frogs is very difficult. They wisely hide quickly and completely at the approach of any human being. Naturalists usually count as many frogs as they can in a small area and then multiply the answer to decide how many there are likely to be in a larger area. This is only what you would call an educated guess, but it is the best that can be done. It is safe to say there are tens of millions of frogs on earth today at the least. No matter how many there are now, it is doubtless far fewer than there were before people began to take up so much space and use so much water.

Africa and South America seem to have most of the world's frogs. Both continents have ideal frog weather all year and large expanses of jungle where cities have not yet been built.

Cuban arrow poison frog (actual size)

FROGS

Throughout most of the time for which we have a written record—which is called history—people have had a pretty low opinion of frogs. This i hard to understand. After frogs do not attack or eat people. They do not a or eat the things peo need for food.

8.

The Frog in Fact and Fiction

Throughout most of the time for which we have a written record—which is called history—people have had a pretty low opinion of frogs. This is hard to understand. After all, frogs do not attack or eat people. They do not attack or eat the things people need for food. Frogs do not destroy the plants people rely on, and frogs do not transmit diseases to people. Frogs are small and shy, for the most part defenseless, and only too glad to leave us alone. Yet they help us by consuming harmful insects in great numbers and by providing a food source in themselves. You would expect such a creature to be regarded with affection or at least appreciation. Instead, all over the world, people have for ages looked down on the peaceful, helpful frog as ugly and stupid at best.

One of the earliest written references to frogs is in the Bible story of Moses.

Moses asked the Pharaoh (king) of Egypt to let Moses' people leave that country, where they were being held as slaves. When Pharaoh refused, the Bible says the God of Moses sent upon Egypt, among other things, a "plague of frogs." This simply means that untold numbers of the little creatures overran everything and got in everyone's way. While this must have been annoying, it was not especially dangerous (except to the frogs), and Pharaoh did not give in.

Worse was to follow, and in the end Pharaoh did let Moses' people leave. None of it, of course, was the fault of the frogs. Then or later, though, people may have decided frogs had to be evil because in this case they were involved with so much distress.

Many people elsewhere in the world also thought frogs were magical in a sinister sort of way. In Africa and in Europe frogs, dead and alive, were used to cast spells that were believed to cure or cause all kinds of things from freckles to fevers.

Other people of long ago went to the opposite extreme and held frogs to be gods. In ancient Rome and among Indians in North America it was believed that killing a frog god would bring on rain.

As time went on and people learned more about the real world around them, the study of frogs received serious attention.

In Italy, not long after the American Revolution of 1776, a doctor named Luigi Galvani was examining a dead frog one day. He touched the frog's lifeless legs with connected pieces of copper and zinc wire, and the legs kicked as though alive. Many years later another Italian, Count Alessandro Volta, recognized that electricity had caused the reaction. It was Count Volta who invented the device we know as a battery.

In 1831 an Englishman named Charles Darwin set out on a five-year voyage aboard the ship *Beagle*. His travels took him to South America and remote islands in the Pacific Ocean. He found birds and animals there that were quite different from those he had grown up with in England. While similar to the English varieties, these birds and animals had special features of appearance or behavior particularly suited to help them survive in their part of the world.

Among them was a frog, little more than an inch long, with a very pointed nose. Darwin observed that the males gathered eggs laid by the females and carried them inside their bodies until completely formed baby frogs hatched and popped out of the father's mouth. Darwin had never seen anything like that among frogs before. It was one of the observations that led him to decide that life on earth is ever-changing, that plants and animals develop from place to place and age to age in ways that help their kind survive as conditions around them change. This became known as the theory of evolution and has been accepted by most scientists.

In the twentieth century frogs have been studied in great detail by so many people that merely listing their names could fill a small book. In fact, if you decide to take up a career in

Darwin's frog

just about any branch of life science, one of the first things you will likely have to study will be the common frog.

With so many people studying them, you would suppose that by now we would know all there is to know about these little animals, but this is not the case. Many questions about even the most familiar kinds of frogs remain unanswered. For instance, not until 1987 did researchers recognize that frogs have special protectors, called peptides, in their skin to help ward off major infections. This discovery may be important in work with human infections.

And new families of frogs are still turning up. In 1983 scientists exploring remote flat-topped mountains in South America found several kinds of frogs no one had even guessed were there. These posed a whole new set of questions and possibilities.

Perhaps the best-known frogs in the world are not real frogs at all but the familiar storybook frogs of which you have likely read or heard. Some of the stories deal with frogs as they truly are, but most are just fanciful tales. Either way they are interesting and can show us much about people's attitudes toward frogs over time.

The single best-known frog story in the world must be that of the Frog Prince (or Princess). It has been told to children virtually everywhere for hundreds and hundreds of years. The details change with the country and age in which it is told, but the basic tale is always the same.

In this story a human being is put under a spell by an evil witch or magician and turned into a frog. To break the spell, the frog must find a person who will love it enough to perform some special deed of courage or magic. The story ends happily when this is done and the frog is transformed back into a wonderful human being.

The moral, or lesson, of these stories seems to be that it is important to love people for their character rather than for their looks, which can be misleading. This is good advice, but it is sad to note that frogs have so often been used by storytellers all over the world as an example of something so ugly it takes rare courage to love one.

You may recognize the name of Mark Twain, who became famous for his still-popular books about two American boys, Tom Sawyer and Huckleberry Finn. The first story Mark Twain ever published, though, was "The Celebrated Jumping Frog of Calaveras County," which told of events surrounding a frog-jumping contest.

There really is a Calaveras County in California, not far from San Francisco, and they really do have frog-jumping contests there. In fact, such contests are regularly held in many places all over the world, including Mr. Twain's hometown of Hannibal, Missouri.

In these contests each frog makes three jumps, one right after another, and the total distance is measured. The frog that jumps the greatest distance wins. In some cases frog contestants have posted scores of twenty feet or more.

With all the story-telling and writing and observing of frogs it is not amazing to find people borrowing the word *frog* for uses other than the familiar animal.

A florist's frog is a glass or wire device placed in the bottom of a dish or vase to hold cut flowers upright.

A violinist's frog is a little piece on the end of a violin bow.

A railroader's frog is a grooved piece of iron used where one track crosses another to let the train pass smoothly over the junction.

Most dictionaries list still more examples.

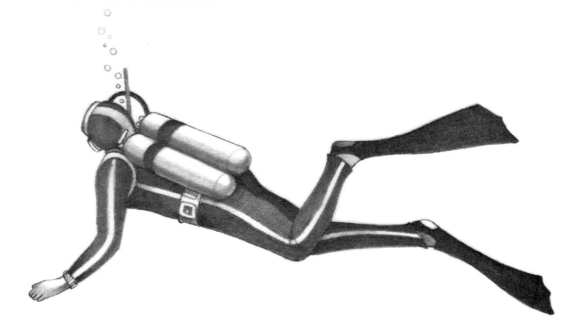

Some uses of the word *frog* you hear more often than others, perhaps depending on what you have been up to lately.

Maybe you have recently played a game of *leapfrog* with your friends.

If you have been swimming, maybe you used the *frog kick,* moving your legs with a froglike action to propel yourself through the water.

Maybe you have seen a movie or television program about *frogmen.* That term originated in World War II when divers were specially trained and equipped so they could move quickly and quietly underwater.

Sometimes a person will cough and then say, "I had a *frog in my throat,"* meaning something small and unimportant had briefly gotten in the way. Or someone might refer to a child as "just a tad"—short for tadpole—meaning a young person with a lot of growing yet to do.

For a shy, quiet animal, the frog certainly manages to find its way into a lot of conversations.

9.
Of Frogs and Folks

*I*t is not possible to generalize neatly about frogs. We cannot say, "Frogs are green," because some frogs are bright orange. We cannot say, "Frogs are smooth," because there are hairy frogs. We cannot even say, "Well, for sure all frogs have long, sticky tongues," because there are those tongueless frogs that live at the bottom of lakes. For virtually *every* accepted rule of "frogness" there is an exception somewhere. This is one of the reasons why frogs are so fascinating to study.

One especially curious feature is that, what with all the variation among them, frogs have *something* in common with just about *every* other animal on earth. They have internal organs similar to those of mammals, and they breathe air, but as babies they have gills and breathe as fish do. They have webbed feet as do ducks and geese and the platypus. Like snakes and lizards, frogs have the trait of shedding an outgrown skin. And with all of those, frogs share an ongoing need for clean water in abundance.

Although these fascinating frogs have been around for millions of years, we terribly smart human beings still do not entirely understand how they have managed such survival success. One reason is that for a long time "studying" frogs consisted of little more than cutting up dead ones to see what they were like on the inside. Only recently have we begun to observe the habits and habitats of living frogs while leaving the animals undisturbed.

Certainly all those centuries of silly attitudes toward frogs complicated our efforts to understand them.

Frogs are not mysterious evil spirits. If you do or do not have freckles and/or warts, frogs had nothing to do with it either way.

Frogs are not magical gods. If your part of the world is suffering from flood or drought, frogs living or dead will not change a thing.

And as for kissing a frog, all that will do is terrify the poor little creature.

Frogs are a marvelous, amazing part of our marvelous, amazing world—and the future of both depends on your continuing curiosity as well as your continuing care.

Selected Bibliography

Blair, W. Frank, *et al. Vertebrates of the United States.* New York: McGraw-Hill, 1957.

Burton, Maurice. *Encyclopedia of Reptiles, Amphibians and Other Cold-Blooded Animals.* London: Octopus Books, Ltd., 1975.

Cochran, Doris M. *Living Amphibians of the World.* New York: Doubleday, 1961.

Dickerson, Mary C. *The Frog Book.* New York: Dover, 1969.

Freedman, Russell, and Moriss, James E. *The Brains of Animals and Man.* New York: Holiday House, 1972.

Grzimek, Bernhard. *Grzimek's Animal Life Encyclopedia.* Vol. 5, *Fishes 2 & Amphibians.* New York: Van Nostrand & Reinhold, 1974.

Hughes, Carol, and Hughes, David. "Teeming Life of a Rain Forest." *National Geographic* 163, No. 1 (January 1983): 49–65.

Parker, Sybil P., ed. *Synopsis and Classification of Living Organisms,* Vol. 2. New York: McGraw-Hill, 1982.

Simon, Hilda. *Frogs and Toads of the World.* Philadelphia and New York: J.B. Lippincott, 1975.

Wood, Gerald L. *Animal Facts and Feats: A Guinness Record of the Animal Kingdom.* New York: Doubleday, 1972.

Zahl, Paul A. "Nature's Living Jumping Jewels." *National Geographic* 144, No. 1 (July 1973): 130–146.

Index

Throughout this book the common English-language names for animals have been used. Professional naturalists use Latin scientific names to identify particular species accurately. Scientific names do change from one generation to another as more information becomes available. In the following index, current scientific names are given beside the common names.